UNDERSTANDING
VERBAL &
EMOTIONAL
ABUSE

BIBLE STUDY

HOPE FOR THE HEART BIBLE STUDIES

June Hunt

ROSE PUBLISHING/ASPIRE PRESS

Peabody, Massachusetts

ROSE PUBLISHING/ASPIRE PRESS

Hope For The Heart Bible Studies
Understanding Verbal & Emotional Abuse Bible Study

Copyright © 2017 Hope For The Heart
All rights reserved.
Published by Aspire Press, an imprint of
Hendrickson Publishers Marketing, LLC
P. O. Box 3473
Peabody, Massachusetts 01961-3473 USA
www.HendricksonRose.com

Get inspiration via email, sign up at
www.aspirepress.com

The views and opinions expressed in this book are those of the author(s) and do not necessarily express the views of Aspire Press, nor is this book intended to be a substitute for mental health treatment or professional counseling.

The information in this resource is intended as guidelines for healthy living. Please consult qualified medical, legal, pastoral, and psychological professionals regarding individual concerns.

For more information on Hope For The Heart, visit www.hopefortheheart.org or call 1-800-488-HOPE (4673).

Printed in the United States of America
010517VP

CONTENTS

About This Bible Study

THANK YOU. Sincerely. Thanks for taking the time and making the effort to invest in the study of God's Word with God's people. The apostle John wrote that he had "no greater joy than to hear that my children are walking in the truth" (3 John 4). At HOPE FOR THE HEART, our joy comes from seeing God use our materials to help His children walk in the truth.

OUR FOUNDATION

God's Word is our sure and steady anchor. We believe the Bible is *inspired* by God (He authored it through human writers), *inerrant* (completely true), *infallible* (totally trustworthy), and the *final authority* on all matters of life and faith. This study will give you *biblical* insight on the topic of verbal and emotional abuse.

WHAT TO EXPECT IN THIS BIBLE STUDY

The overall flow of this topical Bible study looks at verbal and emotional abuse from four angles: Definitions, Characteristics, Causes, and Biblical Steps to Solution.

- The **DEFINITIONS** section orients you to the topic by laying the foundation for a broad understanding of verbal and emotional abuse. It answers the question: What does it mean?

- The **CHARACTERISTICS** section spotlights various aspects that are often associated with verbal and emotional abuse, giving a deeper understanding to the topic. It answers the question: What does it look like?

- The **CAUSES** section identifies the sources of verbal and emotional abuse. It answers the question: What causes it?

- The **BIBLICAL STEPS TO SOLUTION** sections provide action plans designed to help you—and help you help others—deal with verbal and emotional abuse from a scriptural point of view. It answers the question: What can you do about it?

The individual sessions contain narrative, biblical teaching, and discussion questions for group interaction and personal application. We sought to strike a balance between engaging content, biblical truth, and practical application.

GUIDELINES

Applying the following biblical principles will help you get the most out of this Bible-based study as you seek to live a life pleasing to the Lord.

- **PRAY** – "Unless the LORD builds the house, the builders labor in vain" (Psalm 127:1). Any progress in spiritual growth comes from the Lord's helping hand, so soak your study in prayer. We need to depend on God's wisdom to study, think, and apply His Word to our lives.

- **PREPARE** – Even ants prepare and gather food in the harvest (Proverbs 6:6–8). As with most activities in life, you will get out of it as much as you put into it. You will reap what you sow (Galatians 6:7). Realize, the more you prepare, the more fruit you produce.

- **PARTICIPATE** – Change takes place in the context of community. Come to each session ready to ask questions, engage with others, and seek God's help. And "do everything in love" (1 Corinthians 16:14).

- **PRACTICE** – James says, "Do not merely listen to the word, and so deceive yourselves. Do what it says" (James 1:22). Ultimately, this Bible study is designed to impact your life.

- **PASS IT ON!** – The Bible describes a spiritual leader who "set his heart to study the Law of the LORD, and to do it and to teach his statutes and rules" (Ezra 7:10 ESV). Notice the progression: *study . . . do . . . teach.* That progression is what we want for your journey. We pray that God will use the biblical truths contained in this material to change your life and then to help you help others! In this way, the Lord's work will lead to more and more changed lives.

OUR PRAYER

At HOPE FOR THE HEART, we pray that the biblical truths within these pages will give you the hope and help you need to handle the challenges in your life. And we pray that God will reveal Himself and His will to you through this study of Scripture to make you more like Jesus. Finally, we pray that God's Spirit will strengthen you, guide you, comfort you, and equip you to live a life that honors Jesus Christ.

A Note to Group Leaders

"Do your best to present yourself to God as one approved, a worker who does not need to be ashamed and who correctly handles the word of truth."

2 TIMOTHY 2:15

THANK YOU for leading this group. Your care and commitment to the members doesn't go unnoticed by God. Through this study, God will use you to do His work: to comfort, to encourage, to challenge, and even to bring people to saving faith in Christ. For your reference, we've included a gospel message on page 12 to assist you in bringing people to Christ. The following are some helpful tips for leading the sessions.

TIPS FOR LEADERS

- PRAY – Ask God to guide you, the members, and your time together as a group. Invite the group members to share prayer requests each week.

- PREPARE – Look over the sessions before you lead. Familiarize yourself with the content and find specific points of emphasis for your group.

- CARE – Show the members you are interested in their lives, their opinions, and their struggles. People will be more willing to share if you show them you care.

- LISTEN – Listen to the Lord's leading and the members' responses. Ask follow-up questions. A listening ear is often more meaningful than a good piece of advice.

- GUIDE – You don't have to "teach" the material. Your role is to *facilitate group discussion*: ask questions, clarify confusion, and engage the group members.

BEFORE THE FIRST MEETING

Schedule

- Determine the size of the group. Keep in mind that people tend to share more freely and develop genuine intimacy in smaller groups.

- Pick a time and place that works well for everyone.

- Decide how long each session will run. Sessions shouldn't take more than an hour or hour and a half.

- Gather the group members' contact information. Decide the best method of communicating (phone, text, email, etc.) with them outside of the group meeting.

Set Expectations

- CONFIDENTIALITY – Communicate that what is shared in the group needs to stay in the group.

- RESPECTFULNESS – Emphasize the importance of respecting each other's opinions, experiences, boundaries, and time.

- PRAYER – Decide how you want to handle prayer requests. If you take prayer requests during group time, factor in how much time that will take during the session. It may be more effective to gather requests on note cards during the sessions or have members email them during the week.

AT THE FIRST MEETING

Welcome

- Thank the members of your group for coming.

- Introduce yourself and allow others to introduce themselves.

- Explain the overall structure of study (Definitions, Characteristics, Causes, and Biblical Steps to Solution), including the discussion/application questions.

- Pray for God's wisdom and guidance as you begin this study.

LEADING EACH SESSION

Overview

- Summarize and answer any lingering questions from the previous session.

- Give a broad overview of what will be covered in each session.

How to Encourage Participation

- **PRAY.** Ask God to help the members share openly and honestly about their struggles. Some people may find it overwhelming to share openly with people they may not know very well. Pray for God's direction and that He would help build trust within the group.

- **EXPRESS GRATITUDE AND APPRECIATION.** Thank the members for coming and for their willingness to talk.

- **SPEAK FIRST.** The leader's willingness to share often sets the pace and depth of the group. Therefore, it is important that you, as the leader, begin the first few sessions by sharing from your own experience. This eases the pressure of the other members to be the first to talk. The group members will feel more comfortable sharing as the sessions progress. By the third or fourth session, you can ask others to share first.

- **ASK QUESTIONS.** Most of the questions in the study are open-ended. Avoid yes/no questions. Ask follow-up and clarifying questions so you can understand exactly what the members mean.

- **RESPECT TIME.** Be mindful of the clock and respectful of the members' time. Do your best to start and end on time.

- **RESPECT BOUNDARIES.** Some members share more easily than others. Don't force anyone to share who doesn't want to. Trust takes time to build.

Dealing with Difficulties

- You may not have an answer to every question or issue that arises. That's okay. Simply admit that you don't know and commit to finding an answer.

- Be assertive. Some people are more talkative than others, so it is important to limit the amount of time each person shares so everyone has a chance to speak. You can do this by saying something like: "I know this is a very important topic and I want to make sure everyone has a chance to speak, so I'm going to ask that everyone would please be brief when sharing." If someone tries to dominate the conversation, thank them for sharing, then invite others to speak. You can offer a non-condemning statement such as: "Good, thank you for sharing. Who else would like to share?" Or, "I'd like to make sure everyone has a chance to speak. Who would like to go next?"

- Sometimes people may not know how to answer a question or aren't ready to share their answer. Give the group time to think and process the material. Be okay with silence. Rephrasing the question can also be helpful.

- If someone misses a session, contact that person during the week. Let them know you noticed they weren't there and that you missed them.

WRAPPING UP

- Thank the group for their participation.

- Provide a brief summary of what the next session will cover.

- Encourage them to study the material for the next session during the week.

- Close in prayer. Thank God for the work He is doing in the group and in each person's life.

We are grateful to God for your commitment to lead this group. May God bless you as you guide His people toward the truth—truth that sets us free!

"If [your gift] is to lead,
do it diligently."

Romans 12:8

FOUR POINTS OF GOD'S PLAN

The gospel is central to all we do at Hope For The Heart. More than anything, we want you to know the saving love and grace of Jesus Christ. The following shows God's plan of salvation for you!

#1 GOD'S PURPOSE FOR YOU IS SALVATION.

God sent Jesus Christ to earth to express His love for you, save you, forgive your sins, empower you to have victory over sin, and to enable you to live a fulfilled life (John 3:16–17; 10:10).

#2 YOUR PROBLEM IS SIN.

Sin is living independently of God's standard—knowing what is right, but choosing what is wrong (James 4:17). The penalty of sin is spiritual death, eternal separation from God (Isaiah 59:2; Romans 6:23).

#3 GOD'S PROVISION FOR YOU IS THE SAVIOR.

Jesus died on the cross to personally pay the penalty for your sins (Romans 5:8).

#4 YOUR PART IS SURRENDER.

Place your faith in (rely on) Jesus Christ as your personal Lord and Savior and reject your "good works" as a means of earning God's approval (Ephesians 2:8–9). You can tell God that you want to surrender your life to Christ in a simple, heartfelt prayer like this: "God, I want a real relationship with You. Please forgive me for my sins. Jesus, thank You for dying on the cross to pay the penalty for my sins. Come into my life and be my Lord and Savior. In Your holy name I pray. Amen."

WHAT CAN YOU EXPECT NOW?

When you surrender your life to Christ, God empowers you to live a life pleasing to Him (2 Peter 1:3–4). Jesus assures those who believe with these words: "Very truly I tell you, whoever hears my word and believes him who sent me has eternal life and will not be judged but has crossed over from death to life" (John 5:24).

DEFINITIONS OF VERBAL & EMOTIONAL ABUSE

"Teach me your way, LORD; lead me in a straight path because of my oppressors. Do not turn me over to the desire of my foes, for false witnesses rise up against me, spouting malicious accusations."

PSALM 27:11–12

"Y ou're worthless!" "You'll never amount to anything!" "I wish you had never been born!" Words like these in childhood can wound the heart for a lifetime.

And further wounding takes place in adulthood when "control" is the name of the game. Threats like, "If you leave me, I'll hurt the children!" or "I've taken the keys— you're not going anywhere!" are both emotionally and verbally abusive and are ways of maintaining control in relationships.

Abuse can also be perpetrated without a word—whether with degrading looks, obscene gestures, or threatening behaviors. These actions inflict immense pain and impede emotional growth. You don't have to allow an abuser to make you feel worthless. Jesus says that God not only knows each and every sparrow, but He also knows you intimately and considers you to be of great worth.

"Are not five sparrows sold for two pennies?
Yet not one of them is forgotten by God.
Indeed, the very hairs of your head
are all numbered. Don't be afraid;
you are worth more than many sparrows."
LUKE 12:6–7

In this session, we'll look at definitions of verbal and emotional abuse, as well as brainwashing.

Write from the Heart

Imagine the world *without* verbal and emotional abuse. What would it look like? How would it be different than our world today?

How would your life and your past and those of your family and friends be different?

What Is Emotional Abuse?

Emotional abuse is the unseen fallout of all other forms of abuse: physical, mental, verbal, sexual, and even spiritual abuse.

Although abuse such as bullying, neglect, or rejection can be emotionally painful, people often minimize the importance of emotions. Yet with deeply wounded people, their feelings can be the driving force behind their choices and central to their identity. Emotional abuse strikes at the very core of who we are, wearing away our sense of worth, crushing our confidence and our spirit.

The Bible says . . .

> *"A cheerful heart is good medicine, but
> a crushed spirit dries up the bones."*
> PROVERBS 17:22

- *Emotional abuse* is any ongoing, negative behavior used to control or hurt another person.

  - Emotional abuse ranges from consistent indifference to continual belittling of character.

  - All forms of abuse—emotional, verbal, mental, physical, spiritual, and sexual—damage a person's sense of dignity. All forms of abuse wound the spirit of a person and, therefore, are emotionally abusive.

  - Proverbs, the book of wisdom, says:

    "A crushed spirit who can bear?" (Proverbs 18:14).

- *Emotional abuse* or "psychological mistreatment" scars the spirit of the one abused.

  - The damage from emotional abuse can last far longer than damage from any other kind of abuse. A broken arm will soon heal; a broken heart takes much longer.

  - After extended periods of emotional abuse, many victims lose hope, feeling that life is not worth living.

  - The Bible says that:

    "Hope deferred makes the heart sick" (Proverbs 13:12).

- *Emotional abuse* can be passive-aggressive.

  - Passive-aggressive abuse is a means of indirect, underhanded control.

  - Passive-aggressive abusers express their anger through nonassertive, covert behavior.

  - In an attempt to gain control, they often use manipulation as a means of placing themselves in a position of dependence. Then, with underlying anger, they become faultfinders of the people on whom they depend.[1]

  - Passive-aggressive abusers need to recognize and resolve their very real anger and take to heart God's warning:

    "Do not be quickly provoked in your spirit, for anger resides in the lap of fools" (Ecclesiastes 7:9).

Emotional abuse strikes at the very core of who we are.

- *Emotional abuse* can be either overt or covert rejection.[2]

  - *Overt rejection* conveys the message that a person is unwanted or unloved (as when one is belittled as a child).

  - *Covert rejection* takes place in subtle ways that may or may not be intended to cause harm by the perpetrator (as when one is ignored as a child).

  - Jesus said that He will not reject those who come to Him:

    "Those the Father has given me will come to me, and I will never reject them" (John 6:37 NLT).

The Story of Tamar: Overt and Covert Rejection

Read 2 Samuel 13:1–29. Notice the responses of Tamar, Absalom (her brother), and David (her father). How did Tamar respond to the abuse (v. 19)? How did Absalom respond (v. 20, 22–29)? And how did David respond (or fail to respond) to Tamar and to Amnon (v. 21)?

OVERT REJECTION	COVERT REJECTION
Tamar, daughter of King David, was raped by her half brother Amnon, and then was openly and blatantly despised and shunned by him.	Their father, King David, indirectly rejected Tamar by failing to execute justice on her behalf when he refused to hold Amnon accountable for his sin against Tamar. David, in essence, let his son off the hook by totally ignoring the sexual violation of his daughter.

While the Bible doesn't use the term *emotional abuse*, it does instruct us how to treat one another. The Bible details numerous attitudes and actions we should have toward each other. If we follow these guidelines, we can avoid being abusive toward anyone.

"Do nothing out of selfish ambition or vain conceit, but in humility consider others better than yourselves. Each of you should look not only to your own interests, but also to the interests of others."

PHILIPPIANS 2:3–4

Abuse means mistreatment: the destructive misuse of something or someone.

What Is Verbal Abuse?

Verbal abuse is a form of overt emotional abuse. A skilled woodsman wields his ax carefully, chopping repeatedly on a precise spot until the targeted tree falls. This lumberjack takes pride in controlling himself and his weapon, never striking a careless blow. Likewise, a verbal abuser uses his tongue as a weapon to hack away at another person. This abuser is skilled in his ability to strike a blow—wielding words that caustically cut heart and soul.

- *Verbal abuse* is the systematic, ongoing use of harmful words or a sharp tone in an attempt to control or dominate another person.

- *Verbal abuse* is always destructive.

  "Your tongue plots destruction; it is like a sharpened razor, you who practice deceit" (Psalm 52:2).

- *Verbal abuse* injures the feelings of others with reviling, insulting, or contemptuous words.

  The Hebrew word for revile is *gadaph*, from a root word that means "cut" or "wound."[3]

  Jesus endured insults during his crucifixion:

  "When they hurled their insults at him, he did not retaliate; when he suffered, he made no threats. Instead, he entrusted himself to him who judges justly" (1 Peter 2:23).

- *Verbal abuse* often seeks to injure the reputation of others, using tactics such as backbiting, barbs, or belittling talk, and strategies such as slander, slurs, and lies.

  "You love evil rather than good, falsehood rather than speaking the truth" (Psalm 52:3).

Write from the Heart

It is important to define terms and understand that emotional abuse is *abuse*. Verbal abuse is *abuse*. As mentioned earlier, there is often a tendency to minimize emotions. This can lead to minimizing the pain of the abuse.

Why do you think the seriousness of verbal and emotional abuse is often *minimized*?

....

....

....

....

....

....

Read Proverbs 12:18. What effect can words have on people?

....

....

....

....

....

What Is Brainwashing?

Many prisoners of war have succumbed to brainwashing—an effective tactic used in psychological warfare. This term refers to a systematic, forcible indoctrination that puts pressure on prisoners to relinquish their beliefs and accept opposing beliefs.

Unfortunately, you don't have to be in a prisoner of war camp to be brainwashed. Your captor could be a significant member of your own family or a new set of acquaintances. In whatever circumstance brainwashing occurs, the damage can be devastating, systematically wearing away your sense of self-worth and confidence, causing you to distrust yourself and even to lose touch with reality.

"Those people are zealous to win you over, but for no good. What they want is to alienate you from us, so that you may have zeal for them."

GALATIANS 4:17

Tactics Employed by Those Who Brainwash Others

VERBAL BRAINWASHING	
INTIMIDATION	Implying that your failure to comply with all demands or to adopt all the abuser's attitudes or beliefs will result in severe consequences.
INDOCTRINATION	Repeatedly implanting messages contrary to your presently held values or beliefs.
DISCREDITING	Mocking or dismissing your beliefs, perceptions, ideas, and goals; belittling your "outside" family and friends who disagree with the abuser.
DEGRADING	Engaging in name-calling, insults, ridicule, and humiliation.
LABELING	Claiming that your thoughts are childish, stupid, or crazy.

EMOTIONAL BRAINWASHING	
ISOLATION	Depriving you of all outside sources of emotional and social support.
INDUCED EXHAUSTION	Keeping you up late, interrupting your sleep, causing sleep deprivation, wearing you down physically or emotionally.
EXCESSIVE COMPLIANCE	Militantly enforcing trivial demands.
IGNORING	Withdrawing emotional support but later denying the withdrawal.
FORGETTING	Intentionally failing to keep promises and agreements.
EXPLOITING	Using you or someone close to you for selfish interests or gain.

Write from the Heart

Read Psalm 147:3. God cares about the abuse and suffering in our lives. As you begin this study, list some examples of abuse (overt or covert) that you or someone you know have experienced that you would like to bring before the Lord for healing and recovery.

....

....

....

....

....

....

....

....

....

....

....

....

Discussion/Application Questions

1. What are some common misconceptions about abuse, abusers, and victims of abuse.

2. Addressing abuse is no easy task. What are some concerns you have about addressing abuse? What barriers keep people from experiencing the healing and restoration they need?

3. 1 Peter 2:23 says, "When they hurled their insults at him, he did not retaliate; when he suffered, he made no threats. Instead, he entrusted himself to him who judges justly." Jesus endured insults and numerous other forms of abuse and suffering. What does it mean to you to know that Jesus knows and understands abuse?

    ....

    ....

    ....

    ....

    ....

    ....

4. Read Psalm 34:18. What does this Bible verse mean for you and for those who have experienced verbal and emotional abuse? Try memorizing this verse in the coming week by writing it out and posting it where you'll see it often.

    ....

    ....

    ....

    ....

    ....

    ....

SESSION 2

CHARACTERISTICS OF VERBAL & EMOTIONAL ABUSE

"Do not let any unwholesome talk come out of your mouths, but only what is helpful for building others up according to their needs, that it may benefit those who listen."

EPHESIANS 4:29

The Power of Words

Words possess immense power. Through a word, God created the world. Through The Word, Jesus Christ, who was made flesh (John 1:1, 14), God saved the world. Words can be life-giving as well as life-threatening. They can be life-giving by inspiring people to be all they are meant to be or life-threatening by destroying a person's hopes and dashing their dreams. Ultimately, words move from being positive to being abusive when they hurt hearts and harm relationships.

The Bible says . . .

> *"The tongue has the power*
> *of life and death."*
> PROVERBS 18:21

In this session, we'll look at examples of verbal abuse (and also nonverbal abuse) and the effects of abuse on individuals.

Turn to the book of James in your Bible. James writes about the power of words ("the tongue"). Read James 3:1–12 and then answer the following questions.

How does James describe the tongue?

....

....

....

....

....

....

How would you summarize James' teaching on the effects of our words and how we should speak to one another?

....

....

....

....

....

....

....

....

....

How we speak to one another matters. James reminds us that our words can have a big impact on others—they can hurt and they can heal. And just think, we speak thousands of words every day! So we need to ask ourselves: How are my words affecting others? How are the words of others affecting me?

Words can hurt and words can heal.

Here is short list of examples of words that hurt and words that heal.

WORDS THAT HURT	WORDS THAT HEAL
Attacking a Person's Identity *"You're incompetent."*	**Addressing a Person's Action** *"You did something wrong."*
Silencing *"Shut up!"*	**Discussing** *"Please, we need to talk about _____."*
Insulting *"You're worthless!"*	**Complimenting** *"Your life has tremendous value."*
A Negative Picture of the Past *"You've always been a failure."*	**A Positive Picture of the Past** *"You've matured a lot over the years."*
A Negative Picture of the Present *"You can't do anything right."*	**A Positive Picture of the Present** *"You're very good at _____."*
A Negative Picture of the Future *"You'll never amount to anything."*	**A Positive Picture of the Future** *"God has a wonderful plan for your life."*

Write from the Heart

Describe a time when you experienced hurtful words or a time when you said hurtful words. What was the impact?

....

....

....

....

....

....

Now describe a time when you experienced healing words or a time when you said something that deeply encouraged another person. What was the impact?

....

....

....

....

....

....

....

....

....

Familiar Faces of Abuse

Abuse wears many faces—faces as varied as the people who give it and receive it. Abuse can be subtle or blatant, quiet or loud, smooth or abrasive. But with all its differences, abuse is either verbal or nonverbal in delivery, and it impacts your personal and social life.

As you look over the following examples of verbal and nonverbal abuse, place a check mark (√) by the ones you have experienced.

Verbal Abuse

- O Accusing
- O "Advising" excessively
- O Backbiting
- O Badgering
- O Bashing because of gender, race, or religion
- O Belittling
- O Betraying confidences
- O Blame-shifting
- O Brainwashing
- O Breaking promises
- O Bullying
- O Complaining
- O Controlling conversations
- O Criticizing unjustly or excessively
- O Deceiving
- O Degrading
- O Demanding false confessions
- O Demanding that unrealistic expectations be met
- O Demeaning family members
- O Denying that abuse ever occurred
- O Denying that the abuse is wrong
- O Destroying credibility
- O Dictating orders
- O Disgracing
- O Gossiping or slandering
- O Humiliating publicly

Verbal Abuse *(cont.)*

- O Insulting
- O Interrupting constantly
- O Laughing at abusive behavior
- O Lying or truth twisting
- O Making fun of someone
- O Making negative comparisons to others
- O Making racial slurs
- O Manipulating another's reality
- O Minimizing what is wrong
- O Mocking or ridiculing
- O Name-calling
- O Playing mind games
- O Scapegoating
- O Shaming publicly
- O Swearing
- O Teasing publicly about sensitive areas
- O Terrorizing
- O Threatening
- O Threatening suicide in order to control
- O Twisting Scripture
- O Undermining other relationships
- O Using coarse talk
- O Using put-downs
- O Violating the context of conversations
- O Wounding with sarcasm
- O Yelling or screaming

Nonverbal Abuse

- O Abandoning family
- O Acting deceptively
- O Acting overly suspicious
- O Arriving late as a form of control
- O Being chronically irresponsible
- O Being excessively jealous
- O Betraying family, friends, coworkers
- O Brandishing weapons
- O Changing rules or expectations continually
- O Committing adultery
- O Damaging property
- O Driving recklessly
- O Excluding others
- O Favoring others
- O Forcing an abortion
- O Forcing sex/sexual abuse
- O Giving condescending looks
- O Giving excessive gifts to manipulate
- O Giving sneering looks
- O Giving unsolicited "help" to manipulate
- O Hanging up the phone on someone
- O Hiding things
- O Hitting and assaulting physically
- O Ignoring or giving someone "the silent treatment"
- O Interfering with another's work
- O Interrupting another's sleep

Nonverbal Abuse *(cont.)*

- O Intimidating physically or with threatening gestures
- O Invading another's personal space
- O Isolating from family
- O Making insulting gestures
- O Making unwanted visits
- O Manipulating children
- O Monitoring another's phone calls, mail, texts, email
- O Neglecting others
- O Ostracizing
- O Overindulging in order to control
- O Playing cruel tricks
- O Prohibiting another's decision making
- O Prohibiting the positive friendships of others
- O Prohibiting the private conversations of others
- O Refusing to leave when asked
- O Refusing to listen
- O Refusing or failing to validate another's feelings
- O Rejecting one's own child
- O Slamming doors and drawers
- O Stalking
- O Stealing or embezzling
- O Sulking, pouting, "pity parties"
- O Walking away as a power play
- O Withdrawing emotionally
- O Withholding deserved compliments/credit
- O Withholding finances

Write from the Heart

We live in a broken world where it's easy to become accustomed to suffering and even abuse, to view it as normal or even acceptable. Look back over the verbal and nonverbal abuse checklists. How many items did you check for each list? Is the total number surprising to you? Which ones have come to seem "normal" to you?

Read Psalm 31:7, 20–22. What does God do for those who are afflicted?

Methods of Controlling

To gain covert control and personal power, the passive-aggressive, emotionally abusive person will use some (or all) of the following.[4]

FOSTERING CHAOS	Controlling others by intentionally leaving work and projects incomplete.
TELLING LIES OR HALF-TRUTHS	Controlling others with unjustified excuses for not fulfilling commitments.
INVALIDATING	Controlling others by telling them they are wrong, or they misinterpreted what they saw or heard, or that they are overreacting.
PROCRASTINATING	Controlling others by intentionally missing deadlines, thus displaying no regard for the negative impact on others.
BEING CHRONICALLY LATE	Controlling others by keeping people waiting.
BEING AMBIGUOUS	Controlling others by sending mixed messages, leaving others in a wake of confusion about what was said or what was meant.
INSTRUCTING	Controlling others by offering unsolicited advice on a continual basis.
BEING PASSIVELY INDIFFERENT	Controlling others by giving the impression that their concerns are heard and important, but then disregarding them.
PROTECTING AND HELPING	Controlling others by extending help with the intention of causing a sense of indebtedness.
BEING A "QUICK-CHANGE ARTIST"	Controlling others by changing the subject and diverting attention from conversations that feel personally threatening.
WITHHOLDING AFFIRMATION	Controlling others by failing to give deserved compliments and deserved credit.
CROSSING BOUNDARIES	Controlling others by taking advantage of those with little or no personal boundaries.

The Cost of Abuse

There is always a price to be paid for pain, a loss to be incurred by the recipient of abusive words and hurtful gestures. The cost is often unseen—an extensive, inner deprivation that can continue to damage a person for a lifetime.

"The tongue that brings healing is a tree of life,
but a deceitful tongue crushes the spirit."
PROVERBS 15:4

Victims of Abuse May Experience:

Loss of...		Increased...
clear conscience	⇨	guilt or shame
faith	⇨	fear
freedom	⇨	vigilance
friendship	⇨	isolation
happiness	⇨	emotional flatness
hope	⇨	despair
inner peace	⇨	distress
optimism	⇨	pessimism
pride	⇨	self-hatred
security	⇨	desire to escape
self-assurance	⇨	anxiety
self-confidence	⇨	self-consciousness
self-perception	⇨	self-criticism
self-respect	⇨	self-destruction
self-worth	⇨	self-doubt
trust	⇨	distrust

Write from the Heart

As you look over the cost of abuse, which ones stand out to you?
How has abuse impacted you or someone you know?

Discussion/Application Questions

1. Read Proverbs 12:25. Who has been a constant source of encouragement in your life? What *healing words* have they spoken to you? How might you thank them for their encouraging words and for how they've impacted your life?

....

....

....

....

....

....

2. Now read Galatians 6:2. After thinking about a person who has impacted your life in a positive way, there may be someone whose life you could impact. Who can you encourage? What could you say to build them up?

....

....

....

....

....

....

3. Finally, read Proverbs 31:8. Verbal and emotional abuse directed toward the most vulnerable—the young, the aging, or the helpless—is especially cruel. If you were to witness such abuse toward a child, an aging parent or grandparent, or someone with disabilities, what steps could you take to secure their protection? To what extent would you go?

Notes

"Do not let any unwholesome talk come out of your mouths,
but only what is helpful for building others up according to
their needs, that it may benefit those who listen."
Ephesians 4:29

CAUSES OF VERBAL & EMOTIONAL ABUSE

"I say to God my Rock, 'Why have you forgotten me?
Why must I go about mourning, oppressed by
the enemy?' My bones suffer mortal agony as
my foes taunt me, saying to me all day long,
'Where is your God?'"

PSALM 42:9–10

Bringing Your Questions to God

"How can he be so cruel?"

"How can she be so insensitive?"

"Why would he talk that way?"

These are real questions that victims of abusers wonder or ask.

In fact, even the writers of the Bible asked God these kinds of questions when they experienced abuse. Consider Psalm 42:9–10. David was experiencing verbal abuse (taunting, in this case) from his enemies. David was honest before the Lord with his questions and how the abuse was affecting him.

Consider also the prophet Habakkuk. Look how the book that bears his name begins: "How long, LORD, must I call for help, but you do not listen? Or cry out to you, 'Violence!' but you do not save? Why do you make me look at injustice? Why do you tolerate wrongdoing? Destruction and violence are before me; There is strife, and conflict abounds. Therefore the law is paralyzed, and justice never prevails. The wicked hem in the righteous, so that justice is perverted" (Habakkuk 1:2–4).

Habakkuk asks the two questions that may be the most often asked of people who are experiencing abuse or any kind of suffering: *How long?* and *Why?*

This session looks at the causes of abuse. It asks, "Why is this happening?" David and Habakkuk modeled this honest questioning before the Lord. They didn't ignore their questions or stuff their emotions, but they brought it all to God. Likewise, it is important to bring your honest questions to the Lord.

Write from the Heart

Read Psalm 42:9–10. In your own words, describe how the writer is feeling.

....

....

....

....

....

What difficult questions, experiences, or emotions do you want to tell God about? What needs to be said?

....

....

....

....

....

....

....

....

The Background of Abusers

The Childhood Feelings of Abusers

It's common for people who've lived with abuse to lash out and use the same abusive techniques on others. People who rely on abusive techniques to control others usually felt singled out as children. They felt that they were different in several of these areas:

- Too short or too tall

- Too fat or too thin

- Too dark or too light (skin color)

- Physical features too large (nose, ears, feet)

- Physical features unwanted (freckles, acne, bad teeth, hair color)

- Athletically challenged (awkward or uncoordinated)

- Academically challenged (learning disabilities, ADD, or ADHD)

- Physically challenged (disabilities, poor eyesight, hearing problems, or speech difficulties)

Predisposing Influences in the Childhood of Abusers

Not all children who experience abuse become abusers; however, *most abusers have been abused* in one way or another. This raises the question: "Why do some children become abusers while others do not?" Certain factors predispose children to make particular choices about how they respond to their experiences.

Temperament

- The child is willful and assertive.

- The child is confident and forceful.

- The child lacks compassion and empathy for others.

- The child exerts power and control over peers.

Personality

- The child is aggressive and impulsive.

- The child is competent and secure.

- The child has an inflated ego and a sense of entitlement.

- The child is competitive and dominates relationships.

Environment

- The child experiences some form of abuse within the home.

- The child spends excessive, unsupervised hours watching violent videos and TV programs.

- The child forms the belief that being mean to others is the best form of self-protection.

- The child is unable to express anger and frustration safely at home.

Write from the Heart

Those who have endured abuse may have an inaccurate view of who they are in God's eyes because they've been told or treated like they are worthless. Maybe you have experienced this. Read the Bible verses listed below and write down a few words about each as a reminder of your value in God's eyes.

- **1 John 3:1**

  I am..
  ....
  ....

- **Isaiah 43:4**

  I am..
  ....
  ....

- **Psalm 32:1**

  I am..
  ....
  ....

- **Psalm 139:13–18**

  I am..
  ....
  ....

- **Ephesians 1:4–6**

  I am..
  ....
  ....

Three Paths to Travel

Many children are impacted by abusive treatment. Some take the path of succumbing to abuse and defining themselves by that abuse. Others take the path of rising above abuse and defining themselves by positive character-building values. Still, others wonder, "Why did I have to travel down this path?" You may not know the exact answer for some time, but you can know that as long as you continue to entrust your life to the Lord, He will direct your path each step of the way, and you can be an overcomer.

"In this world you will have trouble.
But take heart!
I have overcome the world."
JOHN 16:33

1. The Path of Victims

- Children internalize abusive experiences.

- Children blame themselves for the abuse.

- Children feel deserving of abuse.

- Children seek out abusers who look strong.

- Children remain victims of abusers.

2. The Path of Abusers

- Children internalize abusive experiences.

- Children blame others for the abuse.

- Children feel that others are deserving of abuse.

- Children seek out the weak in order to look strong.

- Children become abusers.

3. The Path of Overcomers

- Children initially internalize their abusive experiences, but later externalize them.

- Children initially blame themselves or others for the abuse, but later forgive all involved in the abuse.

- Children initially feel deserving of abuse, but later feel deserving of loving, trusting relationships.

- Children initially seek out abusers or victims, but later seek out well-adjusted people.

- Children initially remain victims or become abusers, but later reject both roles and become emotionally healthy.

You can be an overcomer!

Fear

You might be wondering, "Why do adults who are being abused continue to stay in abusive relationships?"

One major reason is fear. Isaiah 21:4 says, "My heart falters, fear makes me tremble." Instilling fear is a powerful weapon used to control another person. One effective strategy that instills fear is the use of demeaning messages, such as verbal threats to inflict physical harm. Another fear tactic is to leave or to withdraw emotional support.

The basic underlying fear, however, is the fear of not having the three basic needs met—the needs for love, significance, and security.[5] Yet the Lord wants us to turn from fear to faith and to trust Him to meet our deepest needs.

*"Fear of man will prove to be a snare,
but whoever trusts in the LORD is kept safe."*

PROVERBS 29:25

Write from the Heart

Think about the abuse and suffering that you or someone you know has endured. Who or what did you (or they) typically run to? What role did fear play in the reaction?

The Root Cause of Abusive Relationships

Healthy relationships are those in which the people involved have a clearly-defined sense of their own identities. Without a clear understanding of who we are and of the worth God has given us, it is hard to maintain functional, ongoing relationships that enrich everyone involved. A relationship will not always be smooth, but it can provide a safe, trusting environment in which there is no fear of intimacy and each person knows how to communicate personal needs and desires to the other.

Unhealthy relationships generally reflect an inability to understand and work within appropriate boundaries. Since unhealthy boundaries are almost always the result of being raised in some variation of a dysfunctional family, the likelihood that children raised in such families will develop healthy boundaries is limited.

The pain from not having their God-given needs for love, significance, and security[6] met in childhood carries over into each subsequent relationship—in which they expect, or insist, that these needs be met.

WRONG BELIEF OF VICTIMS	RIGHT BELIEF OF VICTIMS
I am responsible for the way others treat me. I deserve to be mistreated because, at my very core, I am a bad person. Therefore, bad things should happen to me.	I realize that I have been living a lie, believing that I am to blame for being mistreated and believing that my happiness will come from a human relationship.
If I would just be a better person, people would treat me better. I don't have a choice about being mistreated. I must be doing something wrong or I wouldn't be treated this way.	I have a choice about being around anyone who mistreats me. I don't want to have a false loyalty to anyone who abuses me. Nor do I want to have the false expectation that if I can just change, the abuse will stop.
If I just try harder to do what is expected, I can make things better. If I can't, maybe I deserve to be unhappy.	I will no longer live for the approval of others but will rely on the Lord to meet my inner needs—because my value and worth come from Him, and He loves me unconditionally. Only the Lord can meet all my needs.

"Am I now trying to win the approval of human beings, or of God? Or am I trying to please people? If I were still trying to please people, I would not be a servant of Christ."

GALATIANS 1:10

WRONG BELIEF OF ABUSERS	RIGHT BELIEF OF ABUSERS
I am not responsible for the way I treat others; they are to blame. If people wouldn't make me mad, I wouldn't treat them badly. They are the ones who should change, not me.	I realize that I am responsible for the way I respond to others. No one deserves to be belittled, mocked, disrespected or put down.
There's nothing wrong with me. I'm doing them a favor by pointing out and attacking their bad behavior.	No matter how people act toward me, how I act toward them is my choice. God has given me the power, through His Holy Spirit within me, to treat everyone with love and respect.
People just need to accept me the way I am.	I do not need to try to control people because God is in control, and He is the only one who can meet my deepest needs.

"His divine power has given us everything we need for life and godliness through our knowledge of him who called us to his own glory and goodness. Through these he has given us his very great and precious promises, so that through them you may participate in the divine nature and escape the corruption in the world caused by evil desires."

2 PETER 1:3–4

Write from the Heart

Read what Jesus said in Luke 6:45. Our words reveal our hearts. Now think about the last argument you had. If someone who witnessed it were to list three observations about how you handled yourself—and the words you used—what would those observations be? What would the observations reveal about your heart?

(1) ....

....

....

....

(2) ....

....

....

....

(3) ....

....

....

....

Discussion/Application Questions

1. Today, a lot of communication occurs through texts, emails,
   videos, and social media. How have these technologies changed
   the way we speak to (and treat) each other for good and for bad?

   ....

   ....

   ....

   ....

   ....

   ....

2. Think about your upbringing and culture. What did your parents,
   peers, and culture teach you—good or bad—about how you
   should speak to others? What messages did you hear—explicitly
   or implicitly—about how to handle abuse toward yourself or
   others? How do those messages still influence you today?

   ....

   ....

   ....

   ....

   ....

   ....

3. It's often been said, "Hurt people hurt people." How have you seen hurtful experiences in childhood lead to difficulties and more hurtful experiences in relationships later in life?

4. Read Psalm 46:1–2. What encouragement can this passage offer someone who has been or is being abused?

Notes

Notes

"Do not let any unwholesome talk come out of your mouths,
but only what is helpful for building others up according to
their needs, that it may benefit those who listen."
Ephesians 4:29

BIBLICAL STEPS TO SOLUTION

PART 1

"Thanks be to God! He gives us the victory through our Lord Jesus Christ."

1 CORINTHIANS 15:57

How to Rise Above Abuse

Have you ever wished there was some kind of a filter that the words and actions of others—even your *own*—might be poured through to help clearly distinguish between what's *healthy and helpful* and what's *unhealthy and harmful?*

For those on the receiving end of verbal and emotional abuse, many resourcefully find ways to cope—even when their *normal* is not the *norm.* Yet incrementally—little by little—the tendency for many is often to just *give in* and *give up*, allowing behaviors that are unhealthy.

The final three sessions of this study focus on solutions. Remember, God provides the power needed to rise above abuse and move toward a place of emotional health. With His help, you can overcome past abuse and defeat present abuse.

But you may also want to take a careful and honest examination of your own words and actions that may disclose your own guilt—those times you have been guilty of damaging the emotional health of others by careless words or inconsiderate actions. So as you move toward solutions, you want to both overcome the abuse you have endured and also seek God's help so you can stop being verbally and emotionally abusive towards others.

During this session, you'll take an inventory to assess how loving your words are and then look at some practical steps to overcome verbal and emotional abuse.

With God's help, you can overcome past abuse and defeat present abuse.

Write from the Heart

As you think about overcoming past and present abuse and improving how you speak to others, describe how your relationships (at home, work, school, church, etc.) could be healthier. Use this as motivation as you seek God's help in these areas.

....

....

....

....

....

As further motivation, write down a memory when, in obedience to God, you spoke lovingly rather than abusively and it resulted in something positive. What was the outcome and how did it make you feel?

....

....

....

....

....

....

The Language of Love

The best description of love is found in 1 Corinthians 13, often called "The Love Chapter." You may want to highlight it in your Bible, or write it in the front for easy reference. Better yet, memorize it. Your mind will refer to it often. God set the standard for what love is.

Take a moment to read 1 Corinthians 13:4–8 in your Bible.

- Think about your own conversations with those around you—with a stranger, with your coworker, your children . . . with your enemy.

- Gauge the impact of your words through the scriptural filter on the following page. Place a check (√) mark by the ones you would answer yes.

- Evaluate how effectively or ineffectively you speak to others.

- Ask God to reveal any unloving ways—He will help you learn to speak the language of love.

"And now these three remain:
faith, hope and love.
But the greatest of these is love."
1 CORINTHIANS 13:13

The Language of Love Inventory

Love is patient and kind.
- ○ Are my words quick and hasty?
- ○ Are my words kind?

Love is not proud, rude or self-seeking.
- ○ Are my words rude and full of pride?
- ○ Are my words usually all about me and my opinion?

Love is not easily angered, does not envy, does not boast and does not delight in evil.
- ○ Are my words hostile and selfish?
- ○ Are my words arrogant or malicious?

Love always protects, always trusts, always hopes, always perseveres.
- ○ Are my words attacking?
- ○ Are my words creating doubt and despair?

Love keeps no record of wrongs, rejoices with the truth, never fails.
- ○ Are the words I use actually stored-up offenses?
- ○ Are my words reflecting untruth?

Write from the Heart

What does *your* "love language inventory" look like? Were you surprised at how many times you answered *yes*? If so, what needs to change?

List at least two ways you can reflect the character of Christ by changing the way you speak and the way you act toward others.

(1) ....

....

....

....

....

....

(2) ....

....

....

....

....

....

Find Victory Over Verbal Abuse

Perhaps you are regularly exposed to verbally abusive words. Or maybe you were raised in an atmosphere of demeaning talk. Perhaps you are bombarded with inappropriate anger on the job. Those who try to overpower you with verbal attacks may not be as strong and self-assured as they appear. If they express inappropriate anger toward you, realize their assaults are about *them*, not *you*. Their insensitivity stems from a heart suffering from emotional deficits originating in the past, and from their choice to respond to those deficits in abusive ways. Be aware that you may unknowingly have unresolved anger from abuse in your own past that may be magnifying any current abuse.

The following steps look at how a victim can overcome the abuse that they have endured.

Step 1: Identify the Problem.

Identifying verbal abuse might be trickier than first thought without a clear understanding of what it is. Some people disguise their own verbally abusive language by trying to make others feel guilty about something, or by always claiming to be right. Some verbally abuse others by resorting to sarcasm, playing the role of your judge and jury, or by always bringing up the past. Decide that you will no longer tolerate abusive behavior.

"Do not make friends with a hot-tempered person, do not associate with one easily angered, or you may learn their ways and get yourself ensnared" (Proverbs 22:24–25).

Step 2: Understand the Source of the Problem.

So many times those who are verbally abusive have a personal history of enduring abuse or neglect in one way or another as children. Others learned abusive behavior later in life. Regardless, verbal abusers lack sympathy and, for whatever reason, feel justified in their abusive actions. They may not even consider it to be *abuse*. Uncontrolled outbursts of anger are triggered by depression, stress, worry, frustration or insecurity. Although you may be blamed, understand that *you* are not the cause of the abuse others inflict on you.

"The heart of the discerning acquires knowledge; the ears of the wise seek it out" (Proverbs 18:15).

Step 3: Confront the Problem.

Once you identify and understand where the verbal abuse is coming from, find constructive ways to confront the problem. With a caring attitude, let the abuser know that you've been deeply hurt by their abusive behavior. Make it clear that you will no longer tolerate verbal attacks. Communicate the truth without being condemning. Express the consequences that will result from continued verbal attacks, and stick to it. (We'll discuss more details about how to confront and set boundaries in the next session.)

"The wise in heart are called discerning, and pleasant words promote instruction" (Proverbs 16:21).

Step 4: Take Responsibility for Yourself.

The role you play in the management of verbal attacks is vital. You must resist becoming defensive and you must not assume the role of victim. In separating yourself from the behavior of the one who has been abusive, resist the urge to retaliate.

"Do not repay anyone evil for evil. Be careful to do what is right in the eyes of everybody. If it is possible, as far as it depends on you, live at peace with everyone" (Romans 12:17–18).

Step 5: View the Abusive Person from God's Perspective.

When you've been the victim of someone's verbal attacks and emotional abuse, it's a real challenge to maintain a Christian perspective, but it *is* possible. View that person as someone for whom Christ died—just as He died for you. Realize that person has God-given worth—just as you do. Acknowledge that God can change the abuser—just as God changes you. See the person as having needs that God can meet—just as God meets yours.

"My God will meet all your needs according to his glorious riches in Christ Jesus" (Philippians 4:19).

Step 6: Love Unconditionally.

Love is not a feeling; it's a commitment to do the right thing. The "right thing" isn't necessarily what someone wants you to do or tells you to do; it's recognizing another person's genuine needs and trying to help meet those needs as best you can—even when you don't feel like it. Seek God's direction in finding the best ways to convey Christ-like love to others.

"Hatred stirs up dissension, but love covers all wrongs" (Proverbs 10:12).

Step 7: Practice a Purposeful Prayer Life.

A purposeful prayer life is essential. Remember that God cares about you and hears your prayer. He wants to renew every life scarred by the wounds of emotional abuse. God can also open your heart to pray for the emotional healing of the abuser. Thank Him for all He is teaching you and *will* teach you as you obtain victory over verbal and emotional abuse.

"Pray continually; give thanks in all circumstances, for this is God's will for you in Christ Jesus" (1 Thessalonians 5:17–18).

*Love is a commitment
to do the right thing.*

Write from the Heart

Psalm 10 depicts abusers, the abused, and God's activity while abuse is happening. Read the psalm and then answer the following questions.

How does the psalmist describe abusers? The abused?

What does the psalmist say about God while abuse is happening? What does God do for the afflicted?

What does this psalm teach you about how to pray while struggling with abuse and its effects?

Discussion/Application Questions

1. Read Matthew 7:12. How do these words, spoken by Jesus, apply to the words we speak? If you applied this verse to the relationships in your life (family, coworkers, etc.), how would they be different? Give one example.

....

....

....

....

....

....

2. An initial step toward gaining control over verbal and emotional abuse is by viewing others differently—the way God views them. Who do you need to view differently? What would it mean for you to view this person the way God sees them?

....

....

....

....

....

....

3. Describe a situation where you did not reflect the loving spirit you desire to have. To reflect the love of Christ, what would have been a better way to handle the situation?

....

....

....

....

....

....

....

4. Read Jesus' words in Luke 6:28. Think about those who have been verbally or emotionally abusive to you or someone you know. How might you pray for them? (If they don't know the Lord, you can pray for their salvation.)

....

....

....

....

....

....

Notes

"Do not let any unwholesome talk come out of your mouths,
but only what is helpful for building others up according to
their needs, that it may benefit those who listen."
Ephesians 4:29

BIBLICAL STEPS TO SOLUTION

PART 2

*"Let the wise listen and add to their learning,
and let the discerning get guidance."*

PROVERBS 1:5

Boundaries

As you look at practical solutions for dealing with verbal and emotional abuse, one of the most important topics to discuss is the role of boundaries in relationships.

Boundaries are established limits—lines not to be crossed. They are part of daily life. Homes and businesses have property boundaries. Cities, counties, states, and countries have geographic boundaries. Boundaries help define and preserve what is accessible and acceptable and what is not. And just as there are physical boundaries, there are relational and emotional boundaries. These boundaries preserve your emotional health and protect you. It is important to strictly guard who has access to your heart and mind.

The boundaries necessary to protect you from verbal and emotional abuse are easier to enforce when you've established boundaries in every area of your life. How good are your boundaries? Test yourself by answering a few questions:

- Do others often take advantage of you?

- Does someone else expect you to meet all their needs?

- Do certain people expect you to help them, but fail to help you when you need help?

- Does someone at work take advantage of you by piling on you one project after another?

- Do you feel manipulated by someone's lies, half-truths, tardiness, or procrastination?

Perhaps you are nodding an affirming yes to one or more of these questions. When these kinds of emotional boundary breaches occur often, they can be a significant threat to your well-being, growth, and your freedom to serve God.

You can curtail verbal and emotional abuse by developing a plan that prevents you from being controlled by the actions of others. You cannot change someone else, but you *can* change yourself so that the abusive tactics you previously allowed others to use on you are no longer effective. In determining appropriate boundaries, realize these boundaries will help protect your heart.

Write from the Heart

Read Proverbs 4:23. What boundary is stated here? Why is it important to maintain this boundary?

Name some other important boundaries. (They may relate to how you speak to others, what you watch, or how you spend your time.)

....

....

....

....

....

....

....

What are the benefits of having boundaries?

....

....

....

....

....

....

....

....

How to Change Course

There is no specific boundary for every situation. Every experience involving verbal or emotional abuse has its own unique set of circumstances, involving and affecting people of all ages. And every person handles abuse differently. But, it is important to understand that God knows *each* situation and circumstance. With His direction, you can learn how to establish beneficial boundaries. Think of boundary-setting as comparable to having surgery. It can be a painful experience, but the process provides hope for healing. In general, healthy boundaries, established along the following parameters, will change the course of an abusive relationship.

1. State the Boundary.

State clearly, in a conversation or a letter, what you are willing to accept and not accept from the abuser.[7] Communicate your position in a concise, positive way, without apology. Simply state the boundary.

"The one who has knowledge uses words with restraint, and whoever has understanding is even-tempered" (Proverbs 17:27).

2. State the Consequences.

Announce the consequence that you will enforce if the abuser violates your requests. The responding consequence should communicate disengagement from the abuser. You cannot change the abuser's behavior, but you can remove yourself from exposure to unacceptable behavior. Consequences are a normal part of God's plan, that what we sow, we will reap.

"A man reaps what he sows" (Galatians 6:7).

Write from the Heart

What is one boundary you have established (or should establish) in your life? What would the consequences of someone violating that boundary look like? To get started, list the consequences you will carry out if someone verbally abuses you. State those consequences in these terms: "If you violate my boundary by doing _____, I will _____." Consequences will vary from one relationship to another.

3. Enforce the Consequences.

Enforce the consequence every time the abuse occurs. Do not bluff. The abuser needs to know you are going to act consistently on your words. Expect the abuser to test your plan. Typically, the abuser will stop an abusive tactic when it proves to be ineffective. But they might switch tactics and try testing the boundary again . . . and again. Say no to manipulation. Say no to pressure. Say no to control.

"Let your 'Yes' be yes and your 'No' be no" (James 5:12).

4. Do Not Negotiate.

Since verbal abusers do not use words fairly, negotiation will not work. Instead of "talking out" a problem, the abuser will seek to wear you out. Keep your words brief and to the point. Simply state that when the behavior stops, you look forward to a renewed relationship.

For example, you could say:

- "I am not willing to discuss this topic any longer."
- "I have clearly stated what I will not accept."
- "When you are ready to respect my requests, let me know."

"When words are many, sin is not absent, but he who holds his tongue is wise" (Proverbs 10:19).

5. Respond, Instead of Reacting.

Never "react" when your boundary is violated—only respond. Expect your boundary to be violated but respond by detaching yourself from the abuser and enforcing your repercussions. Do not react by crying because of feeling hurt. Do not beg because of feeling fearful. Do not lash back or explode because of feeling frustrated.

"A hot-tempered person stirs up conflict, but the one who is patient calms a quarrel" (Proverbs 15:18).

6. Seek Support.

Solicit the support of one or two wise, objective people to help you through this process. Their input will help you analyze and identify the problem, will help articulate your plan, and will support you as you enforce repercussions.

"Listen to advice and accept instruction, and in the end you will be wise" (Proverbs 19:20).

Write from the Heart

As you consider the steps needed to establish relational boundaries, what concerns do you have? What do you think will happen if you communicate your boundaries and enforce the consequences when those boundaries are violated?

How to Confront

Ignoring abusive behavior won't make it go away. Things won't get better with wishful thinking. Keeping quiet about it out of loyalty will never work.

Although victims of verbal and emotional abuse often feel inadequate and powerless to stop an abusive relationship, appropriate confrontation is often necessary to defuse emotional abuse.

But don't expect change to be easy. It will likely be met with resistance by the abuser. When power is the goal and control is at stake, don't be surprised when an abuser repeatedly changes tactics in an attempt to maneuver around each boundary you set, always looking for some way to put you in a position to be manipulated. To remain silent in such a relationship is not love but fear, and is harmful rather than helpful.[8]

"For the Spirit God gave us does not make us timid, but gives us power, love and self-discipline."
2 TIMOTHY 1:7

Ignoring abusive behavior won't make it go away.

1. Start Educating Yourself.

Emotional abuse may go on for years before victims realize it. Abusers can be calculating and their behavior is often deliberate—designed to control. In some relationships the abuser goes back and forth between harshness and extravagant kindness that draws you back into the relationship.

Once you understand the tactical behavior of the abuser, much of your discouragement will begin to dissipate and you can begin to establish a more level playing field.

"Let the wise listen and add to their learning, and let the discerning get guidance" (Proverbs 1:5).

2. Set Boundaries.

- Communicate that you will not tolerate disrespectful treatment.

  "You are treating me disrespectfully and I will not stay here (or I will not stay on the phone) if it continues."

- Be specific about what behavior is unacceptable.

  "I won't continue to talk with you if you continually interrupt me."

- Refuse to accept excuses and reasons for repeated inconsiderate behavior.

  "You were late again and did not call. From now on if that happens, I'll go about my plans without you."

"Whoever rebukes a person will in the end gain favor rather than one who has a flattering tongue" (Proverbs 28:23).

3. Seize the Moment.

Speak up as soon as the abuser tries to change the subject or twist your words to mean something other than what you intended. Repeat what you actually said and ask the abuser to restate what you said. The abuser is looking for a strong reaction from you, but remain calm. Inform them that you will discuss it at a later time when words can be spoken with more restraint.

"A gentle answer turns away wrath, but a harsh word stirs up anger" (Proverbs 15:1).

4. Seek to Surface the Other Person's Hostility.

When you sense anger in the other person, acknowledge it. Confirm that being angry is permissible and is sometimes justified. A person may need help recognizing the cause of the anger. Simply ask, "What triggered your anger?"

"The purposes of a person's heart are deep waters, but one who has insight draws them out" (Proverbs 20:5).

5. Soften the Confrontation Process.

Confront the behavior, not the person. Without raising your voice, keep it civil by avoiding threats, sarcasm, hostility, put-downs or judgment. Let the person know that you care about them, but do not like what they are doing. If their behavior stems from their anger toward you, invite them to talk to you about it so that you can understand why, but they must stop their present behavior.

"Be completely humble and gentle; be patient, bearing with one another in love. Make every effort to keep the unity of the Spirit through the bond of peace" (Ephesians 4:2–3).

6. Stay in the Present.

Keep your focus on the issue at hand. Do not bring up past problems. The abuser may try to get you off track, but do not allow it. Stay focused.

"Let your eyes look straight ahead, fix your gaze directly before you. Make level paths for your feet and take only ways that are firm. Do not swerve to the right or the left; keep your foot from evil" (Proverbs 4:25–27).

7. Squelch Unrealistic Expectations.

Understand that you cannot *make* the abuser change. Your hope is not in your ability to change a person but in God's ability, so place your hope in God and in His sufficiency. Change will only occur after the abuser admits to having a problem and begins to receive the help and support needed to turn from the problem.

"Blessed are those whose help is the God of Jacob, whose hope is in the LORD their God" (Psalm 146:5).

8. Strengthen Your Relationship with the Lord.

Always look to the Lord for discernment about your relationship, asking Him to give you wisdom, insight, and direction. As you read your Bible, take God at His word in order to renew your mind so that you will not continue to live as a victim. Get involved in biblical community. Let God talk to you through His Word and talk to Him through prayer. Live dependently on Christ, who lives within the believer.

"I have been crucified with Christ and I no longer live, but Christ lives in me. The life I now live in the body, I live by faith in the Son of God, who loved me and gave himself for me" (Galatians 2:20).

Place your hope in God and in His sufficiency.

Write from the Heart

Think about the people in your life—your family, friends, neighbors, coworkers, church community, and the children in your life. Does a particular individual come to mind who you suspect might be a victim of verbal and emotional abuse? Commit to praying for that person.

Ask the Lord to show you some immediate ways you can encourage that person. What can you say to them? What can you do for them? Write down the ideas that come to mind.

Discussion/Application Questions

1. Knowing how to speak to one another can be helpful in establishing boundaries and confronting others. Read Proverbs 27:5–6; Matthew 18:15–17; Ephesians 4:15, 29; Colossians 3:8; James 1:19. What do these passages tell us about how we should speak to one another, especially when confronting others?

   ....

   ....

   ....

   ....

   ....

   ....

2. Think about your family history. What old patterns of verbal and emotional abuse have been resolved? What *used to happen* that no longer happens as the result of setting boundaries?

   ....

   ....

   ....

   ....

   ....

3. Now think about the future of your family. Describe the potential impact of establishing boundaries in your key family relationships.

....

....

....

....

....

....

4. Read Isaiah 41:10. Think of a situation that seemed impossible to confront at the time, but with God's help, you found the courage to do so. What was it? What did God teach you through that experience?

....

....

....

....

....

....

The next session digs deeper into the *emotional* part of abuse. Between now and then, observe your own life and the lives of those around you, and try to detect where boundaries would benefit your emotional health and the emotional health of others.

Notes

"Do not let any unwholesome talk come out of your mouths,
but only what is helpful for building others up according to
their needs, that it may benefit those who listen."

Ephesians 4:29

BIBLICAL STEPS TO SOLUTION

PART 3

"Because of God's tender mercy, the morning light from heaven is about to break upon us, to give light to those who sit in darkness and in the shadow of death, and to guide us to the path of peace."

LUKE 1:78–79 NLT

God Will Heal Your Broken Heart

As you begin this last session on verbal and emotional abuse, you probably have a good idea where your own personal boundaries are crumbling, and you may recognize areas in need of reinforcements. Or maybe you realize that you have never established boundaries at all. But what about the emotional erosion that has already occurred? How can someone *rebuild* after the damage of emotional erosion and abusive accusations have already occurred? What are the solutions for *that*?

No one escapes the pain of a broken heart. In Hebrew, the meaning of the word translated *brokenhearted* is literally "shattered."[9] Many people stumble through life shattered by the effects of emotional abuse. Perhaps this describes you as past insults replay in a never-ending loop in your mind. But take comfort. God mends the brokenhearted and attends to their emotional wounds.

> *"He heals the brokenhearted and*
> *binds up their wounds."*
> PSALM 147:3

In this session, we'll look at steps to promote emotional healing. Then we'll look at steps to overcome being verbally and emotionally abusive to others.

Write from the Heart

By now, you may realize you are well-acquainted with verbal and emotional abuse. What hurtful words do you still remember, and how have those words impacted your life? What residual feelings related to that verbal abuse still need the Lord's healing?

Actions You Can Take toward Healing

The path to healing from emotional abuse is a process that takes time. As you walk with the Lord, ask Him to help you take these actions toward healing.

1. Give Your Heart to the Lord.

Allow Him to be your Deliverer. Acknowledge your inability to heal yourself and accept the fact that God is the source of all growth and healing. Ask the Lord to heal your past pain as you take refuge in Him and draw on His strength.

"The LORD is my rock, my fortress and my deliverer; my God is my rock, in whom I take refuge" (Psalm 18:2).

2. Know that You Are Never Alone.

Realize that everyone occasionally experiences loneliness and pain in life. But thank the Lord that He never leaves you. Build a network of friends who care about you and who will support you both spiritually and emotionally.

"The LORD himself goes before you and will be with you; he will never leave you nor forsake you. Do not be afraid; do not be discouraged" (Deuteronomy 31:8).

3. Search for Truth.

Discern the truth about what has wounded you in the past and what your present struggles are. Search God's Word to find truth and wise counsel to build you up and encourage you. Look for wise counsel from trustworthy people to help you understand and address your situation.

"Guide me in your truth and teach me, for you are God my Savior, and my hope is in you all day long" (Psalm 25:5).

4. Address Your Legitimate Emotional Needs.[10]

Understand that you have three God-given needs: the need for love, significance, and security. When you see yourself through the lens of God's compassion, you can better understand your invaluable worth. Understand that God never withholds His love from you, though you may not have sensed that you were loved by your parents or your spouse.

"You are a forgiving God, gracious and compassionate, slow to anger and abounding in love" (Nehemiah 9:17).

5. Pay Attention to Your Own Feelings and Perceptions.

Understand that the abuse is actual *abuse*. If you felt abused, acknowledge that what happened is unacceptable.

"You will know the truth, and the truth will set you free" (John 8:32).

6. Clear Your Mind of Confusion.

Realize you have been a victim of confusing, mixed messages. You may need to seek help from a safe, trustworthy person to sort through those confusing messages and to distinguish the truth from the lies. Refuse to be confused if the abuser tries to reverse the blame or counters what you are saying.

"God is not a God of confusion but of peace" (1 Corinthians 14:33 ESV).

7. Acknowledge Your Negative Feelings.

Make a list of any negative feelings you may have, such as anger, bitterness, unforgiveness, hate, or revenge. Be honest with God about these feelings; He knows you have them, and He understands why. Ask God to cleanse you from unhealthy, negative feelings and attitudes.

"Cleanse me with hyssop, and I will be clean; wash me, and I will be whiter than snow" (Psalm 51:7).

8. Allow Yourself to Grieve.

Write down all the losses that have occurred in your life. Allow yourself time to grieve those you have not yet grieved.

"There is a time for everything, and a season for every activity under heaven . . . a time to mourn . . . " (Ecclesiastes 3:1, 4).

9. Forgive Your Abuser.

List each offense committed against you by each abuser. As an act of your will, choose to release each offense, the pain it caused, and each abuser into the hands of God.

"Bear with each other and forgive whatever grievances you may have against one another. Forgive as the Lord forgave you" (Colossians 3:13).

10. Realize that Healing Is a Process, Not an Event.

Refuse to look for quick fixes or painless solutions. Involve yourself in activities that will promote healing. You will grow in patience as you embrace the journey of the healing process.

"As an example of patience in the face of suffering, take the prophets who spoke in the name of the Lord. As you know, we consider blessed those who have persevered" (James 5:10–11).

11. Reach Out and Minister to Others.

Ask God for a compassionate heart that is sensitive toward those who have also experienced abuse. Be prepared to share your experience when God brings other victims across your path.

"Praise be to the God and Father of our Lord Jesus Christ, the Father of compassion and the God of all comfort, who comforts us in all our troubles, so that we can comfort those in any trouble with the comfort we ourselves have received from God" (2 Corinthians 1:3–4).

Write from the Heart

After reading through the steps towards healing, which ones seem especially applicable to you right now? Why?

Breaking through the Heart of an Abuser

Maybe you are wondering: *Is restoration even possible for the abuser?* The answer is *yes!* But for change to occur, the loving work of God is necessary in the heart of the abuser.

This section addresses the abuser who wants to change. The following five action steps outline what is required for change to occur to break through the heart and ways of an abuser.

It's important to remember that while restoration and healing are possible for the abuser, this does *not* mean that the abused person should stay in the relationship or try to reconcile with their abuser. Reconciliation should only be pursued once the abusive person *consistently* exhibits the characteristics listed in this section for a significant period of time.

Step 1: Be Honest.

Many abusers have no idea they are abusive. Is it possible that *you* may have been abusive? Are you willing to consider that you may not be in touch with your own emotions because they have been buried or ignored for so long?

"A truthful witness gives honest testimony, but a false witness tells lies" (Proverbs 12:17).

Step 2: Desire to Change.

Give careful thought to *how* you are responding. Here are some do's and don'ts for taking responsibility:

- *Don't* spew pent-up anger on another person.

- *Don't* say, "You're the reason I am so angry" or "I can never please you!"

- *Don't* use harsh, belittling, or sarcastic statements.

- *Don't* withdraw emotionally.

- *Do* understand that feeling angry is not a sin.

- *Do* recognize and admit that you may not know how to handle your anger.

- *Do* realize that you may be using your anger to get your own way.

- *Do* be willing to enlist friends and family members to hold you accountable.

"Search me, God, and know my heart; test me and know my anxious thoughts. See if there is any offensive way in me, and lead me in the way everlasting" (Psalm 139:23-24)

Step 3: Be Reflective.

Examine your situation. Most families will have some issues of control, but some children are subject to methods of power and authority that are more extreme than normal. Usually when a parent is overtly dominating, a child's feelings are stepped on, and personal expression is stifled and an atmosphere of fear invades the family. Although the behavior of the children, when they are grown, may not be the same as the behavior of their offending parents, their emotional focus may cause them to develop the same attitudes of resentment and bitterness they so disliked in their parents.

Ask yourself . . .

- Was anyone in my family overly controlling? Am I still angry about that?

- Do I still harbor resentment toward anyone in my past?

- Have I ever bitterly vowed that I will never exhibit the same behaviors as my parents?

- Do I have a negative focus on one or both parents and still talk about their negative behavior?

- Have I learned to love the parents God gave me in spite of their faults?

  "Love one another. As I [Jesus] have loved you, so you must love one another" (John 13:34).

Step 4: Manage Anger.

People who have difficulty controlling anger usually express it in two ways: *explosive* and *implosive*. If you vent your anger at someone else, your anger is explosive, but if you keep your anger bottled up, your anger is implosive. Explosive anger is outwardly abusive, while implosive anger is inwardly abusive. Both are damaging to relationships. You need to address and express your anger in appropriate, God-honoring ways.

"In your anger do not sin" (Psalm 4:4).

Step 5: Exercise Self-control.

Discover your trigger points.

- Be aware of when you are feeling irritated or aggravated.
- Listen to yourself. Are you behaving badly, performing poorly, or snapping at others?
- Stop and give yourself time to discover the source of anger.

Restrain angry thoughts and actions.

- Turn your thoughts toward Christ: "Lord, may I have Your peace."
- Count to 10 before you respond.
- Walk away and then come back after your feelings are under control.

Choose the right time and the right way to express your feelings.

- Train yourself to keep a lid on your anger until your agitation is calmed.
- If you are angry at another person, ask, "Is there a time when we could talk about something important to me?"
- If you have anger turned inward, talk with a friend and seek an objective view of the situation.

Be aware of your early family background.

- Recall your early family dynamics.
- Did you learn it was not safe to express anger?
- Did you observe that explosive anger was a means of control?

Begin absorbing truth.

- Pray for the Lord to reveal His love for you and reveal to you how He sees you—the person He created you to be.
- Acknowledge that you have God-given worth. Don't let others define who you are.
- Memorize verses about how to handle anger. Begin with Psalm 37:8; Ephesians 4:26; Colossians 3:8; James 1:19–20.

Write from the Heart

Read Psalm 141:3. Describe how your life would change if you prayed this verse regularly.

....

....

....

....

....

....

As you think about the ways in which you may have been verbally or emotionally abusive to others, which of these steps just discussed (honesty, desire to change, reflection, managing anger, and self-control) are particularly applicable to you? Why?

....

....

....

....

....

....

God Will Help
the Sincere Heart

God can transform an abuser. In 1 Timothy 1:12–17, Paul describes how God transformed him from an abuser to an apostle. After reading the passage, answer the following questions.

How does Paul describe himself before and after meeting Jesus? What did Jesus do for him?

....

....

....

....

....

What lessons do you learn about abuse from Paul's transformation?

....

....

....

....

....

....

As you've gone through each session in this study, it may be that God has brought to light a truth that is hard for you to face: you've been guilty of verbal and emotional abuse. You've hurt others with your words and actions. If that's your reality and you want to change, you *can* with God's help. You can change because nothing is too hard for your Creator. You can change because of God's unwavering faithfulness. You can change because of God's transforming power.

CONFESSION	"I admit that my behavior has been wrong and has hurt others."
REPENTANCE	"Relying on God's strength, I want to please Him and will change my behavior."
FORGIVENESS	"God, thank You for Your willingness to forgive me."
ACCEPTANCE	"Jesus, I receive You as my Lord and Savior and give You control of my life."
SUBSTITUTION	"I am willing to give up control of my life in exchange for a new life in Christ."
RESTITUTION	"Lord, reveal the names of those to whom I owe a sincere apology. I will go to them and ask forgiveness for my inappropriate and hurtful behavior."
CLEANSING	"God, thank You for Your promise to cleanse me and remove all my sins."

"If we confess our sins, he is faithful and just and will forgive us our sins and purify us from all unrighteousness."

1 JOHN 1:9

Write from the Heart

God may be bringing to mind an occasion when you hurt someone with your words or actions. If He is, write a confession to Him about the wrongdoing or harm you caused that person—whether recently or in the distant past. Who, if anyone, do you need to apologize to? What other actions may also be necessary to mend the relationship?

Discussion/Application Questions

1. Over the past six sessions, how has your understanding of verbal and emotional abuse changed as a result of this study? What are one or two key takeaways the Lord has revealed to you about verbal and emotional abuse?

....

....

....

....

....

....

2. In thinking about both overcoming the abuse you've experienced or the ways in which you've verbally or emotionally hurt others, what habits need to start, change, or stop concerning these areas?

....

....

....

....

....

....

3. Read 1 Thessalonians 5:9–11. Who in your life needs to be encouraged and "built up"? What are some truths you've learned from this study that can help them?

....

....

....

....

....

....

4. Read 2 Corinthians 1:3–4. As a prayer of praise and gratitude, list the ways God has comforted you and encouraged you through this study and throughout your experiences of verbal and emotional abuse.

....

....

....

....

....

....

....

Endnotes

1. Andre Bustanoby and Fay Bustanoby, *Just Talk to Me* (Grand Rapids: Zondervan, 1981), 148.

2. Charles R. Solomon, *The Ins and Out of Rejection* (Littleton, CO: Heritage House, 1976), 13–25.

3. Francis Brown, S. R. Driver, and Charles Briggs, eds., *Hebrew-Aramaic and English Lexicon of the Old Testament*, electronic ed. (n.p.: 1906).

4. Robert Burney, "Emotional Abuse is Heart and Soul Mutilation," http://www. joy2meu.com/emotional_abuse.html; Scott Wetzler, *Living with the Passive-Aggressive Man*, repr. ed. (1992; repr., New York: Fireside, 1993), 35–37; Harold I. Kaplan and Benjamin J. Saddock, *Synopsis of Psychiatry*, 8th ed. (Baltimore: Williams & Wilkins, 1997), 793–94; Michael Arndt and Clare Dacy, "Healing Emotional Abuse," http:/www.designedthinking.com/Fear/ Abuse/abuse.html.

5. Lawrence J. Crabb, Jr., *Understanding People*, (Grand Rapids: Zondervan, 1987), 15–16; Robert S. McGee, *The Search for Significance*, 2nd ed. (Houston, TX: Rapha, 1990), 27–30.

6. Crabb, *Understanding People*, 15–16; McGee, *The Search for Significance*, 27–30.

7. Susan Forward, *Toxic Parents* (New York: Bantam, 1989), 236–274.

8. Bustanoby and Bustanoby, *Just Talk to Me*, 159–60.

9. Brown, Driver, and Briggs, *Hebrew-Aramaic and English Lexicon*

10. Crabb, *Understanding People*, 15–16; McGee, *The Search for Significance*, 27–30.

HOPE FOR THE HEART
Biblically Based Studies on Everyday Issues
6-Session Bible Studies

CHOOSING FORGIVENESS
Learn how you can be an expression of God's grace by forgiving others and find the freedom He intended you to have.
ISBN: 9781628623840

DEALING WITH ANGER
Have you ever reacted rashly out of anger—and lived to regret it? You can learn to keep your anger under control and learn how to act rather than react.
ISBN: 9781628623871

OVERCOMING DEPRESSION
Can anything dispel the darkness of depression? The answer is yes! Let God lead you through the storm and into the light.
ISBN: 9781628623901

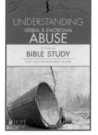

UNDERSTANDING VERBAL AND EMOTIONAL ABUSE
You can learn biblical truths and practical "how to's" for stopping the pain of abuse and for restoring peace in all your relationships.
ISBN: 9781628623932

HANDLING STRESS
Discover biblical approaches to handling stress. God wants to be your source of calm in stressful situations.
ISBN: 9781628623963

FINDING SELF-WORTH IN CHRIST
Learn to leave behind feelings of worthlessness, and experience the worth you have in the eyes of your heavenly Father.
ISBN: 9781628623994